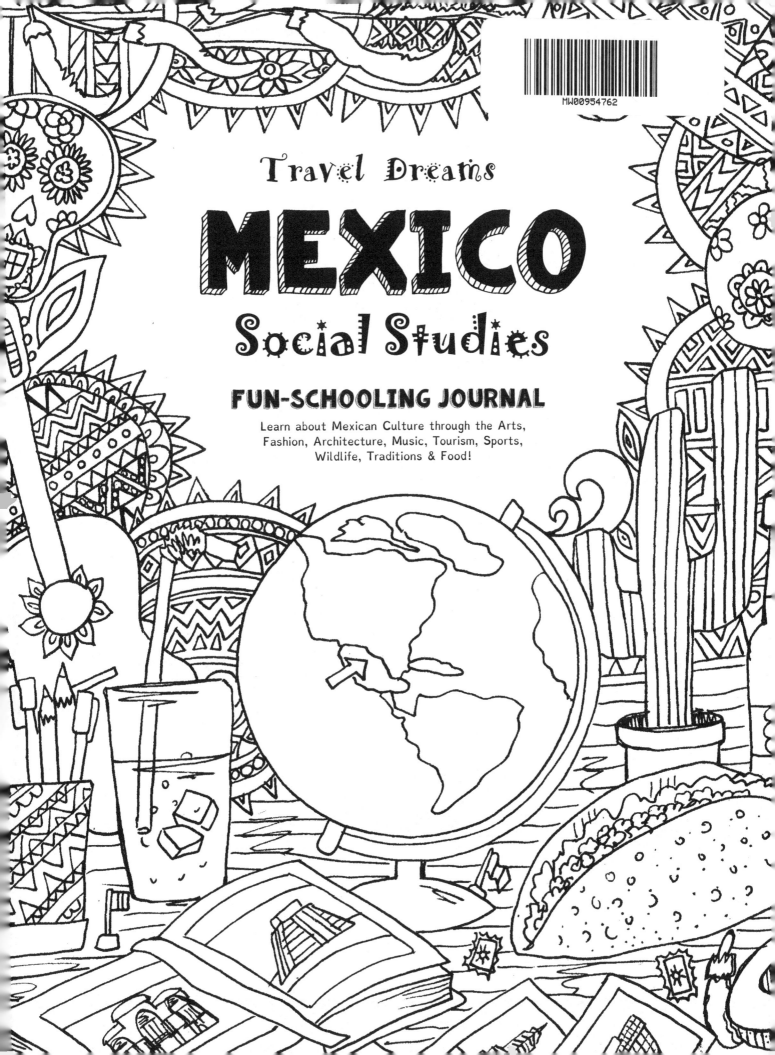

Travel Dreams

MEXICO

Social Studies

FUN-SCHOOLING JOURNAL

Learn about Mexican Culture through the Arts,
Fashion, Architecture, Music, Tourism, Sports,
Wildlife, Traditions & Food!

To hear traditional music from this country listen to

Travel Dreams
Geography

AROUND THE WORLD
IN 14 SONGS

Search for Amazon Product Number: B072C2QXJS

Around the world in 14 songs is a delightful musical tour of the world. Adults and children will enjoy these original instrumental songs that reflect the authentic style of music that originated on all six major continents. Travel to the rhythm and melody of traditional instruments, and enjoy the fun-filled tunes.

The musical journey begins in Ireland, sweeps across Europe, dances through Asia, Africa and then soars over the ocean to Australia and the Caribbean! After an exciting night at a Smoky Mountain bluegrass festival you will enjoy a siesta in Mexico and finally land in Brazil where you will join the festa in Rio-De-Janeiro.

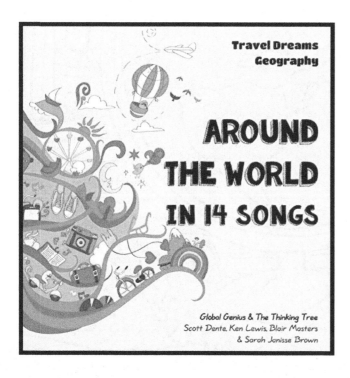

Music has never
been more fun...
or educational!

Travel Dreams

MEXICO

FUN-SCHOOLING
JOURNAL

An Adventurous Approach

Social Studies

Learn about Mexican Culture through the Arts,
Fashion, Architecture, Music, Tourism, Sports,
Wildlife, Traditions & Food!

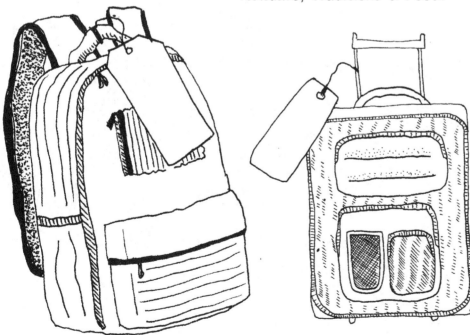

Travel Dreams
MEXICO
FUN-SCHOOLING
Journal

Name:

Date:

Contact Information:

About Me:

Let's Learn!

Topics & Activities You Can Explore With This Curriculum:

- Ethnic Cooking
- Travel
- History of Interesting Places
- How People Live
- Tourism
- Transportation
- Wildlife and Natural Wonders
- Cultural Traditions
- Natural Disasters

- Famous and Interesting People
- Missionary Stories
- Scientific Discoveries
- Fashion
- Architecture
- Plants
- Animals
- Maps
- Language

MEXICO

Travel Dreams Fun-School Journal

You are going to learn about Mexico

Teacher & Parent To-Do List:

- Plan a trip to Mexico or just plan a trip to the library or local bookstore.
- Download Google Earth so your child can zoom in and learn more!
- Choose online videos about Mexico so your child can learn about culture, food, tourism, traditions and history.
- Be prepared to help your child choose an ethnic recipe and shop for the ingredients.

Go to the Library or Bookstore to Pick Out:

- Books about Mexico
- One Atlas or Book of Maps
- One Colorful Cookbook with Recipes from Mexico

DRAW THE COVER OF YOUR BOOKS!

COLOR IN MEXICO ON THE MAP

Zoom into Mexico using Google Earth and explore the wonders of this amazing country!

LABEL THE MAP
Add 15 Interesting Things to this Map!

Write or Draw

Use your Library Books

Popular Foods:	Traditional Clothing:
Draw the Flag:	A Quote or Proverb:
A Historic Event:	A Famous Landmark:

LEARNING TIME

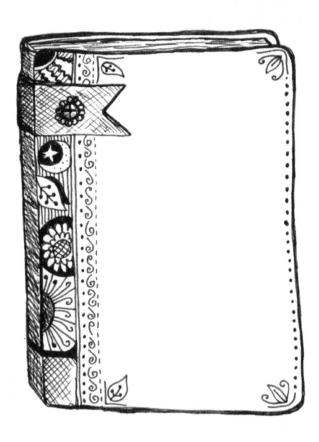

READ A BOOK AND WATCH A VIDEO ABOUT FOOD IN MEXICO:

BOOK TITLE:_____

_____

VIDEO TITLE: _____

_____

WHAT did YOU LearN?

_____
_____
_____
_____
_____
_____

MEXICAN CUISINE

What do Mexicans love to eat?

Can you list 5 of the most popular Mexican dishes?

1. _____
2. _____
3. _____
4. _____
5. _____

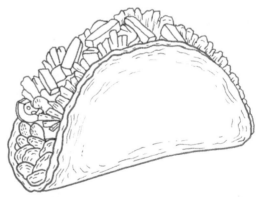

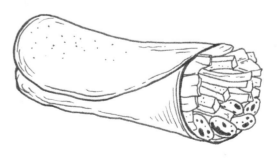

Draw your favorite Mexican food

Find a Recipe From
MEXICO

TITLE:

_____

Ingredients:

_____ _____

_____ _____

_____ _____

_____ _____

_____ _____

Instructions:

_____

_____

_____

_____

_____

_____

_____

_____

Step by Step Food Prep:

1	2
3	4
5	6

21

DRAW THE FOOD THAT YOU PREPARED!

RATE THE RESULTS!
1, 2, 3, 4, 5

Color the words that best describe your food:

DELICIOUS

YUMMY

TASTY

GREAT

DELIGHTFUL

OKAY

BLAH!

GROSS

YUCKY

DISGUSTING

STINKY

ICKY

What to Do in Mexico

Create a **COMIC STRIP** showing your dream adventure!

LEARNING TIME

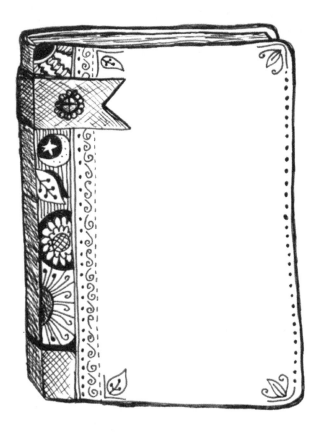

READ A BOOK AND WATCH A VIDEO ABOUT A FAMOUS PERSON

BOOK TITLE:_____

_____

VIDEO TITLE: _____

_____

_____

Write 3 Interesting Biography Facts

_____

_____

_____

_____

_____

_____

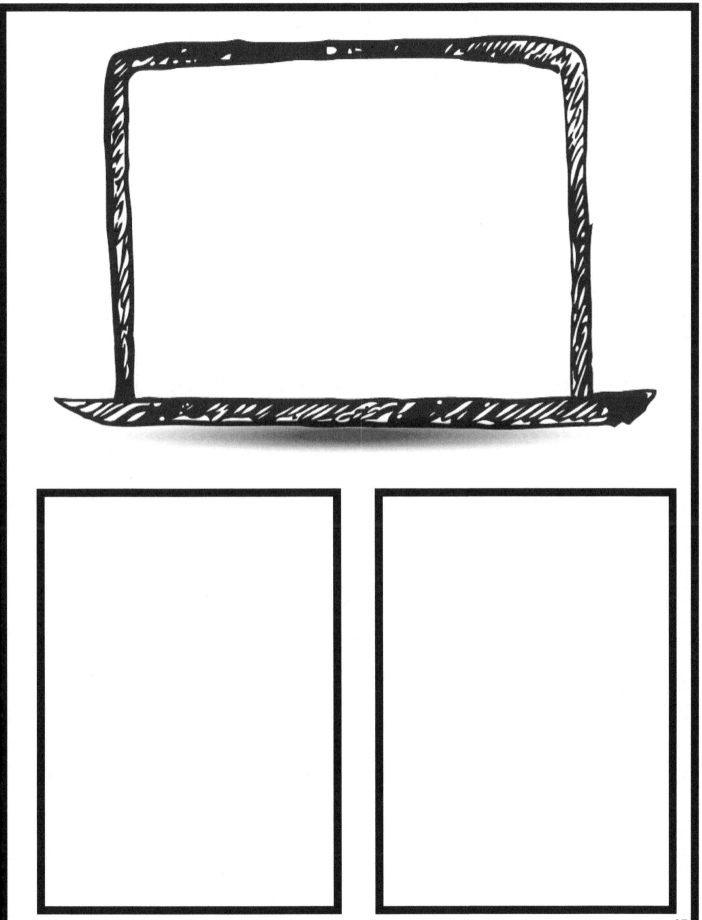

All About Style
MEXICO
Fashion in the City

_____

_____

_____

MODERN STYLES
Draw yourself dressed like a stylish Mexican :

Color The Traditional Costume:

Trace and color this
traditional Female Mexican costume

Trace and color this traditional male Mexican costume

MEXICAN HISTORY

Write about a Historic Event

_____

_____

_____

_____

_____

_____

_____

_____

_____

_____

_____

_____

_____

_____

_____

_____

LEARNING TIME

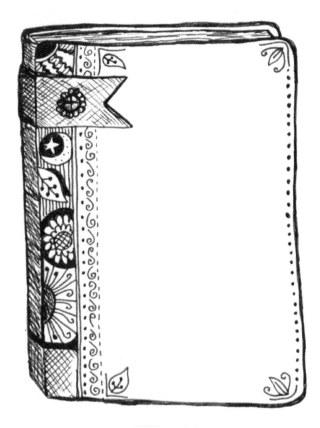

READ A BOOK AND WATCH A VIDEO ABOUT NATURE & WILDLIFE

BOOK TITLE:_____

_____

VIDEO TITLE: _____

_____

_____

Notes:

_____

_____

_____

_____

_____

_____

WHaT ANiMaLS LiVe iN MeXiCo?
CaN yoU LiSt teN?

1. _____

2. _____

3. _____

4. _____

5. _____

6. _____

7. _____

8. _____

9. _____

10. _____

Draw each of the animals

PLANTS IN MEXICO

Can you list ten flowers or trees found in Mexico?

1._____

2._____

3._____

4._____

5._____

6._____

7._____

8._____

9._____

10._____

Draw each of the plants

HISTORY OF MUSIC IN MEXICO

Write about a famous Mexican musician:

_____

_____
_____
_____
_____
_____
_____
_____

What instrument did he/she play?

_____

Can you draw it?

A NATIONAL INSTRUMENT

To hear traditional music from this country listen to
Travel Dreams Geography—Around the World in 14 Songs

Track Number & Song Name:
13-Mexico – The Siesta Sisters

MEXICAN ART & ENTERTAINMENT

Read a book or watch a documentary about art and entertainment in Mexico

Write down 5 interesting things you learned :

1. _____
_____

2. _____
_____

3. _____
_____

4. _____
_____

5. _____
_____

Draw or doodle in Mexican style

Write doWN a quote or a Lyric From a FaMouS MeXicaN poeM or SoNg

_____

_____

_____

_____

_____

_____

_____

_____

_____

_____

_____

_____

_____

_____

HISTORY OF TRANSPORTATION IN MEXICO

Find 3 interesting facts about Mexican transportation

1. _____
_____
_____

2. _____
_____
_____

3. _____
_____
_____

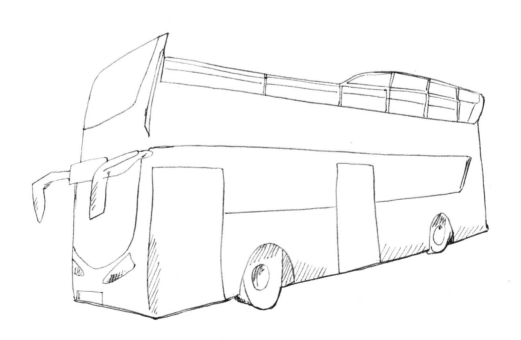

Use your imagination and add something to this picture.

Write a short story about this picture

_____

_____

_____

_____

_____

_____

_____

_____

_____

_____

MEXICAN INVENTIONS

Read a book or Watch a documentary about your Favorite Mexican inventor:

_____

Write down 5 interesting things about his/her life:

1._____
_____

2._____
_____

3._____
_____

4._____
_____

5._____
_____

Write down 3 Mexican inventions that changed the world:

1. _____

2. _____

3. _____

Draw your Favorite Mexican invention

MEXICAN ATHLETES

Read a book or Watch a documentary about your Favorite Mexican Athlete:

_____

Write down 5 interesting things about his/her life:

1. _____
_____

2. _____
_____

3. _____
_____

4. _____
_____

5. _____
_____

DraW a PopuLar MeXican Sport

MEXICAN HOMES

Write about a Family tradition in Mexico

_____

_____

_____

_____

MEXICAN TRADITIONS

Draw some traditional Mexican décor elements

Trace & Color
A TRADITIONAL MEXICAN HOME

Design Your Own
MEXICAN HOME

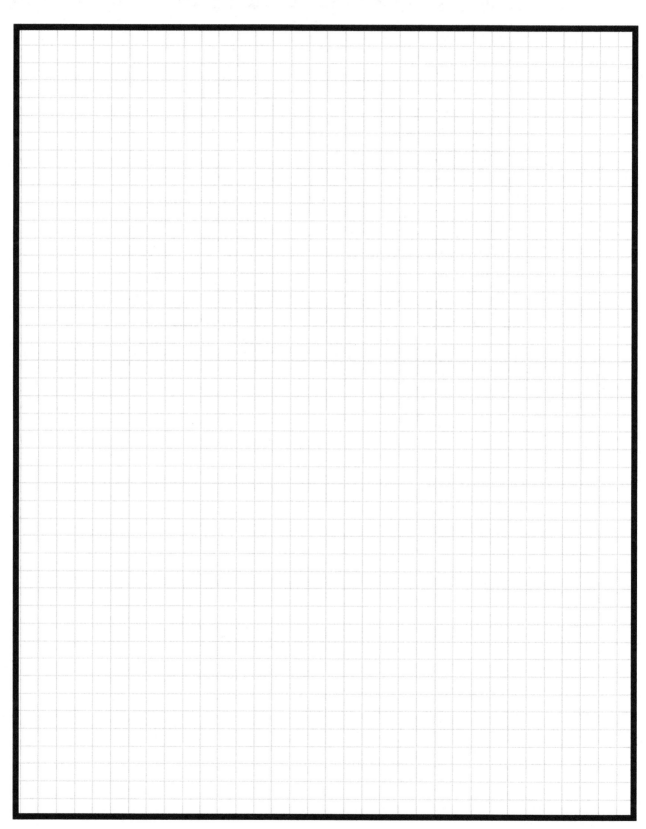

FiND aNd COLOr iN tHe HiddeN objects

LEARNING TIME

READ A BOOK AND WATCH A VIDEO ABOUT TOURISM & TRAVEL

BOOK TITLE:_____

_____

VIDEO TITLE: _____

_____

_____

Notes:

_____

_____

_____

_____

_____

_____

PLAN A TRIP TO THE CAPITAL OF MEXICO

▬▬▬▬▬▬ ▬▬▬▬

Who are you going with?

_____

What are you taking with you?

_____

How long is your trip?

_____

What do you want to see or visit?

_____

56

PLAN YOUR TRIP
What to Do in Mexico City

Five Things to Know when Traveling to
MEXICO

1 _____

2 _____

3 _____

4 _____

5 _____

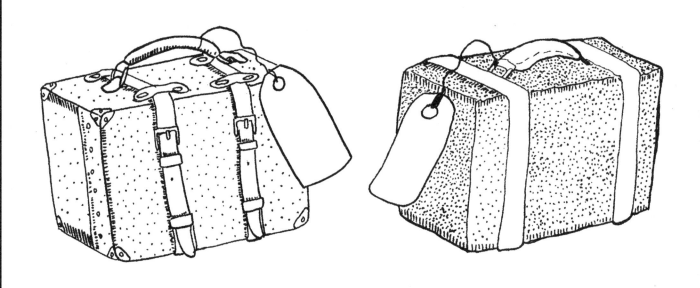

What to Say

Create a COMIC STRIP using six Spanish words or phrases:

CREATIVE WRITING

Write a story about an imaginary trip to Mexico

Illustrate your Story

Do It Yourself
HOMESCHOOL
JOURNALS

BY THE THINKING TREE, LLC

THE Thinking TREE

PUBLISHING COMPANY

Sarah Janisse Brown

ART LOGICAL SCIENCE SPELLING READING COLOR THINKING DRAWING CREATING

Made in the USA
Las Vegas, NV
31 May 2021